**Editor**
Eric Migliaccio

**Managing Editor**
Ina Massler Levin, M.A.

**Editor-in-Chief**
Sharon Coan, M.S. Ed.

**Cover Artist**
Barb Lorseyedi

**Art Coordinator**
Kevin Barnes

**Imaging**
Ralph Olmedo, Jr.

**Product Manager**
Phil Garcia

**Publisher**
Mary D. Smith, M.S. Ed.

# Punctuation Capitalization

## GRADE 2

**Author**

*Michelle Breyer, M.A.*

**Teacher Created Resources, Inc.**
6421 Industry Way
Westminster, CA 92683
www.teachercreated.com

**ISBN: 978-0-7439-3345-2**

©2002 Teacher Created Resources, Inc.
Reprinted, 2008
Made in U.S.A.

# Table of Contents

# Introduction

The old adage "practice makes perfect" can really hold true for your child and his or her education. The more practice and exposure your child has with concepts being taught in school, the more success he or she is likely to find. For many parents, knowing how to help their children may be frustrating because the resources may not be readily available.

As a parent, it is also difficult to know where to focus your efforts so that the extra practice your child receives at home supports what he or she is learning in school.

This book has been written to help parents and teachers reinforce basic skills with children. *Practice Makes Perfect: Punctuate and Capitalize* reviews basic grammar skills for second graders. The exercises in this book can be done sequentially or can be taken out of order, as needed.

The following standards or objectives will be met or reinforced by completing the practice pages included in this book. These standards and objectives are similar to the ones required by your state and school district and are appropriate for second graders.

- The student writes clear, complete, and coherent sentences.
- The student correctly uses and capitalizes the pronoun "I."
- The student identifies and correctly capitalizes the first word in a sentence.
- The student identifies and correctly capitalizes simple proper nouns (e.g., names of people, days of the week, months of the year)
- The student identifies different types of sentences (i.e., declarative (telling), interrogative (questioning), and exclamatory (with emotion) sentences).
- The student correctly capitalizes the greeting and closing of a friendly letter.
- The student uses correct punctuation at the end of sentences (i.e., period, question mark, exclamation point).
- The student uses a comma to separate words in a series.
- The student uses a comma to separate adjectives (describing words) describing the same noun.
- The student uses a comma in the greeting and closing of a friendly letter.
- The student uses a comma to separate dates and to separate city and state.
- The student uses quotation marks in dialogue (speaking) and to identify titles.

## How to Make the Most of This Book

Here are some useful ideas for making the most of this book:

- Set aside a specific place in your home to work on this book. Keep it neat and tidy, with the necessary materials on hand.
- Set up a certain time of day to work on these practice pages to establish consistency; or look for times in your day or week that are less hectic and more conducive to practicing skills.
- Keep all practice sessions with your child positive and constructive. If your child becomes frustrated or tense, set the book aside and look for another time to practice. Forcing your child to perform will not help. Do not use this book as a punishment.
- Help beginning readers with instructions.
- Review the work your child has done.
- Allow your child to use whatever writing instruments he or she prefers. For example, colored pencils can add variety and pleasure to drill work.
- Pay attention to the areas in which your child has the most difficulty. Provide extra guidance and exercises in those areas.

# Introduction *(cont.)*

Exercises are provided for students to practice each rule. There is also a section of mixed practice to work with all of the different rules combined. It is up to the adult to determine which pages are appropriate for his/her student.

Assessments are also provided to help evaluate your student's progress. A Quick Check follows each section of the book. The Quick Check evaluates only the concepts covered in that section. However, the Unit Assessment at the end of the book covers all of the concepts covered throughout the book. This assessment is provided in a Standardized Test format to allow students to practice their knowledge as well as their test-taking skills. An answer key has also been provided (pages 46–48).

Use this section as a handy reference guide to punctuation.

---

**Capitalize the pronoun I:** Yesterday I went to the store.

**Capitalize the first word in a sentence:** My brother has a pet lizard.

**Capitalize Proper Nouns**

    **Names of People:** George Washington

    **Names of Places:** Idaho, New York City, Disneyland

    **Days of the Week:** Tuesday, Thursday

    **Months of the Year:** March, October

    **Titles:** *Free Willy*, *The Aristocats*

**The greeting and closing in a letter:** Sincerely, Dear Sirs, Your friend

**Punctuate the end of a sentence:**

    **A period ends a declarative (telling) sentence:** I like to eat pizza.

    **A question mark ends an interrogative (questioning) sentence:** Will you shut the door?

    **An exclamation point ends an exclamatory (with feeling) sentence:** Look out for that rock!

**Punctuate most abbreviations with a period:** Dr., Mr., Blvd.

**Punctuate with commas:**

    **Use a comma to separate words in a series:** I have red, yellow, and green paint.

    **Use a comma to separate adjectives describing the same noun:** Throw the big, red ball.

    **Use a comma in the greeting and closing of a friendly letter:** Dear Grandma, Sincerely,

    **Use a comma to separate dates:** My birthday is July 12, 1994.

    **Use a comma to separate the city and state:** I live in Carlsbad, California.

**Punctuate with quotation marks:**

    **Use quotation marks around a direct quote (words being spoken):** Kara said, "I love my rat!"

    **Use quotation marks to identify titles of chapters, songs, or poems:** We sang "America."

# I Can Do It!

**Capitalization Rule**: Capitalize the pronoun "I."

Correct each sentence by crossing out and capitalizing the pronoun "I."

1. i can't go to the park today because i didn't clean my room.

2. Today i am going to buy a book, and i will pay with my own money.

3. On Friday i will play in a soccer game, or i will play baseball.

4. Do i have to eat my green beans, or can i just eat my salad?

5. i love the color blue, and i also like red.

Write the pronoun "I" to complete each sentence.

6. _____ like to jump rope, and _____ like to play handball at recess.

7. Can _____ go with Janie, or can _____ go with Sheila to the movies?

8. Today _____ spent one hour doing homework, and _____ finished!

9. Did _____ remember to feed my fish, or did _____ forget?

10. _____ really enjoyed that video game, and _____ know you will, too.

# The I's Have It

**Capitalization Rule**: Capitalize the pronoun "I."

Write the following sentences correctly by capitalizing the pronoun "I."

1. Can i play on the slide today? _____

_____

2. i will come back after i finish my lunch. _____

_____

3. When will i get a turn on the swings? _____

_____

4. i like to dig in the sand before i leave. _____

_____

5. Today i had fun at the park, and i hope to come back. _____

_____

Write a sentence describing what you like to do at the park. Start your sentence with the words "I like to. . . ."

_____

_____

_____

# Start It Off Right

**Capitalization Rule:** Capitalize the first word in every sentence.

Circle the first word in each sentence. Then write the word on the space, using a capital letter.

_____

1. a man named Mr. Hemerson owns the pet shop. _____
_____

2. there are many animals in his shop. _____
_____

3. he has birds, dogs, cats, and snakes in cages. _____
_____

4. my favorite animal is the bunny in the window. _____
_____

5. do you have a favorite pet? _____
_____

Write a sentence to go with each picture of an animal. Be sure to capitalize the first word of each sentence.

1. _____
_____
_____

2. _____
_____
_____

3. _____
_____
_____

# A Capital Idea

**Capitalization Rule:** Capitalize the first word of every sentence.

Match the beginning to the end of each sentence by drawing a line. Then write each sentence on the lines below. Be sure to capitalize the first word of each sentence.

| Beginning | End |
|---|---|
| my dog had | the piano each day. |
| she practices playing | puppies last year. |
| that duck can | how to cook? |
| do you know | swim quickly. |

1. _____

2. _____

3. _____

4. _____

# Quick Check #1

Read each sentence below.  If the sentence is capitalized correctly, write "correct" on the line following the sentence.  If it is capitalized incorrectly, write "incorrect" on the line.  Then cross out and correct any capitalization errors.

1. my mother likes to cook a special dinner each week.

   _____

2. This week I got to pick the menu for our special dinner.

   _____

3. I decided to make tacos with ground beef.

   _____

4. do you like to eat tacos?

   _____

5. we chopped tomatoes and then i grated the cheese.

   _____

6. I shredded the lettuce and put it in a bowl.

   _____

7. When it was dinner time i set the table, and i poured the milk.

   _____

8. we ate our tacos with rice and beans.

   _____

9. Do you have a special dinner that you like to eat?

   _____

10. next week i hope my mother cooks spaghetti!

   _____

# Quick Check #2

Circle the capitalization errors in each sentence. Then write each sentence correctly.

1. i like to pretend that i can travel through time.

2. once i pretended to visit a king and queen.

3. they took me to their castle where i met a dragon.

4. the dragon was friendly, so i named him Norbert.

5. norbert and i flew around the kingdom in the sky.

6. what do you like to pretend?

# What's in a Name?

**Capitalization Rule:** Capitalize proper nouns, such as the names of people.

Choose a name from the box below to complete each sentence. Be sure to capitalize first, middle, and last names.

| | | |
|---|---|---|
| **sheila** | **dane smith** | **zack t. griffin** |
| **christopher** | **hallie wilson** | **maria g.** |

1. I play ball with _____ .

2. Can I go to the movies with _____ .

3. _____ likes to eat ice cream.

4. _____ has a pet parrot.

5. Will you tell _____ that I can't go?

6. I'm going to watch television with _____ .

# That Time of the Year

**Capitalization Rule**: Capitalize proper nouns, such as days of the week and months of the year.

Write a sentence that describes what you do on the days below. Name the day in your sentence, for example, "On Tuesday I. . . ." Capitalize the day of the week.

1. friday

2. wednesday

3. saturday

Circle the days and months in the sentences below. Then write each sentence correctly, using capital letters for the names of the days and months.

1. I had my birthday on a tuesday in december.

2. We will take a trip on a monday in june.

3. I saw a football game on a friday in october.

# Proper Places

**Capitalization Rule:** Capitalize proper nouns, such as specific places with names.

Many places are listed in the box. Some of these places are specific and have a name. These places are proper nouns and should be capitalized. Write the names of these specific places on the lines below. Be sure to capitalize the first letter of each word in a proper noun.

| | | |
|---|---|---|
| river | indiana | mountain |
| alameda street | road | snake river |
| canada | country | mount everest |
| clty | san francisco | king road |
| florida | school | new mexico |
| store | lake michigan | ocean |

1. _____

2. _____

3. _____

4. _____

5. _____

6. _____

7. _____

8. _____

9. _____

10. _____

# Terrific Titles

**Capitalization Rule:** Capitalize proper nouns, such as the titles of books, movies, songs, television shows, and plays.

Rewrite the following sentences, capitalizing the underlined titles that name books, movies, songs, television shows, or plays.

1. Our class went to see <u>the music man</u>. _____

_____

2. We read <u>arrow to the sun</u> to study Native Americans. _____

_____

3. My favorite book is <u>harry potter and the sorcerer's stone</u>. _____

_____

4. <u>snow white</u> is now out on video. _____

_____

5. I like to watch <u>pokemon</u> on Saturday mornings. _____

_____

Name some of your favorite things. Be sure to use capital letters for their titles.

1. favorite book _____

2. favorite movie _____

3. favorite song _____

# Letter Writing

**Capitalization Rules**: Capitalize the first word of a greeting and closing in a letter. Capitalize all proper nouns and beginning of sentences.

Read the letter below. Circle the words that should be capitalized.

november 15, 2002

dear sandra,

i am writing to invite you to my birthday party. The party will be on friday,

december 3, 2002. it will begin a 2:00 P.M. the party will be at calaveras park in carlsbad, california. i hope you will be able to come.

your friend,

molly adler

Practice capitalizing the following greetings and names.

_____

1. dear grandma martha, _____

_____

2. dear aunt teresa, _____

Practice capitalizing the following closings. Be sure to capitalize only the first word of the closing.

_____

1. yours truly, _____

_____

2. sincerely yours, _____

# Quick Check #3

Show what you know about capitalizing proper nouns by filling out the form below.

| | |
|---|---|
| Name (first, middle, and last) | |
| Age | Birthday |
| Today's Date (name of the day, number, and month) | |
| Street Address | |
| City | State |
| Grade Level | Teacher |
| Title of your favorite book | |
| Title of your favorite television show | |
| Best friend (first and last name) | |
| Favorite place to visit | |

# Quick Check #4

Writo tho following sentences, using a capital letter for each proper noun.

1. jasmeet najeed sits next to me at kelly school. _____

_____

_____

2. We go to hope park after school with jason and kaitlin thomas. _____

_____

_____

3. In october the leaves begin to turn red in vermont. _____

_____

_____

4. Can you come to my house to read *goosebumps* on tuesday? _____

_____

_____

5. Mrs. jacobs taught us to sing "this land is your land" on thursday. _____

_____

_____

6. I love to swim with tony and anna in july at the newcastle pool. _____

_____

_____

# Make a Declaration

> **Punctuation Rules**: Sentences end with a punctuation mark. Declarative (telling) sentences end with a period.

Unscramble the words to make a sentence. Be sure to add a capital letter at the beginning and a period at the end.

1. mouse cat the chased a _____

_____

2. ate bag a my sister of chips _____

_____

3. hiker tall hill climbed the the _____

_____

4. my house to came man old an _____

_____

5. the rolled pig pink the mud in _____

_____

6. hanging spider web was there a from its _____

_____

18

# Question Time

> **Punctuation Rules**. Sentences end with a punctuation mark. Interrogative (questioning) sentences end with a question mark.

Write a question that begins with each word below. Be sure to end your question with a question mark.

1. Who

2. What

3. When

4. Where

5. Why

6. How

# Shout It Out!

**Punctuation Rules**: Sentences end with punctuation marks. Exclamatory (with feeling) sentences end with exclamation points.

Write an exclamation to go with each picture. Be sure to end your sentence with an exclamation point.

1.

2.

3.

4.

5.

20

# Shorten It

**Punctuation Rule**: Use a period after most abbreviations.

An abbreviation is a short way to write a word. Write the abbreviation for each of the words below. Use the abbreviations in the box to help you.

| | | |
|---|---|---|
| **Sept.** | **doz.** | **Ave.** |
| **St.** | **Wed.** | **Dr.** |
| **yd.** | **pg.** | **ft.** |
| **Mr.** | **in.** | **yr.** |

1. Street _____

2. yard _____

3. inch _____

4. Wednesday _____

5. Doctor _____

6. Mister _____

7. Avenue _____

8. September _____

9. feet _____

10. dozen _____

# Dear Sir

**Punctuation Rule**: Use a period after most abbreviations.

Circle all of the abbreviations on the envelope below

Mr. Maurice K. Adams
132 S. Masters Rd.
Ste. 100
Encinitas, CA  92024

Dr. Dianne J. Hutchinson
10043 St. Martin Blvd.
Apt. 3206
Boise, ID  45508

Match each abbreviation from the envelope to the word it abbreviates.

1. California _____

2. Boulevard _____

3. Doctor _____

4. Apartment _____

5. Idaho _____

6. Road _____

7. Suite _____

8. South _____

9. Saint _____

10. Mister _____

Which two abbreviations do not have a period? _____

# Quick Check #5

Rewrite the following sentences. Add periods, question marks, and exclamation points where needed.

1. Will Mr Hall see Dr Hay today _____

2. Bill W Hood lives on Baker St _____

3. Look out for that falling tree _____

4. Does Mrs J G Smith have a pet poodle_____

5. We won the game _____

6. Will we play at the park on Hope Ave _____

7. Jr Jones played ball on Conger Blvd _____

# Quick Check #6

Read the letter and envelope below.  Add periods, question marks, and exclamation points where needed.

Dec 3, 2002

Dear Samantha,

   I am writing to invite you to a party for Mrs Allen, our teacher   The party will be on Sat , Dec 11, 2002  It will be held at my house, which is located at 7008 Lantana Ave in Wellmington  The party will start at 2:00  Do you think you can come

   We are planning to surprise Mrs Allen with dessert, games, and a gift for being such a good teacher  Could you please bring some punch and some cups   I hope you can come  This will be the best party ever

Your friend,

Molly S Brown

Molly S Brown

7008 Lantana Ave

Wellmington, CO 80406

Samantha H Sonnich

2437 Hanson Pl

Wellmington , CO  80406

# Lists

> **Punctuation Rule**: Use commas to separate words in a series.

Use the word bank at the bottom of the page to complete each sentence. Be sure to separate each series of words with commas.

1. Would you like _____ _____ or _____ for dinner?

2. I like to play _____ _____ and _____ .

3. I have _____ _____ and _____ crayons.

4. I saw _____ _____ and _____ at the zoo.

5. Is this shape a _____ _____ or _____ ?

6. I practice on _____ _____ and _____ .

| | |
|---|---|
| pizza  pasta  steak | lions  tigers  bears |
| soccer  golf  tennis | triangle  square  circle |
| red  blue  green | Monday  Friday  Sunday |

# The Word Series

**Punctuation Rule**: Use commas to separate words in a series.

Practice using commas in a series by completing the lists below. Be sure your answers are in complete sentences. The first one has been done for you.

1. Name three colors of paint.

   *Three colors of paint are red, blue, and violet.*

2. Name three sports that use a ball.

3. Name three vegetables.

4. Name three animals that make good pets.

5. Name three of your best friends.

# Describing Words

**Punctuation Rule**: Use commas to separate adjectives (describing words) that modify the same noun.

Separate the adjectives in the sentences below by putting commas in the correct places. The first one has been done for you.

1. The friendly, furry, brown dog wagged his tail.

2. My cat has a wet pink tongue.

3. Can Juan bring a sharp new yellow pencil to school?

4. A big shiny new car raced passed our house.

5. Did that big hairy red monster scare you?

6. My sister wore her old torn jeans to school.

7. I love large hot cheese pizza for dinner.

8. Does your dad have a large brown fuzzy mustache?

9. We played with the round blue ball at recess.

10. Some red juicy apples fell from the tree.

# Want a Date?

**Punctuation Rule**: Use a comma to separate the day and year when writing a date.

Practice writing a comma between the day and the year by writing the dates listed below. The first one has been done for you.

| Month | Day | Year | Correctly Written Date |
|-------|-----|------|------------------------|
| 1. March | 2 | 1662 | March 2, 1662 |
| 2. July | 12 | 1994 | |
| 3. June | 22 | 1939 | |
| 4. April | 16 | 2018 | |
| 5. January | 27 | 1785 | |
| 6. May | 26 | 2002 | |

In the following dates, the month is abbreviated. Rewrite each one, placing a period after the abbreviation and a comma after the day.

7. Aug 13 1875 _____   10. Sept 3 2003 _____

8. Oct 31 1998 _____   11. Nov 15 1793 _____

9. Mar 23 2000 _____   12. Jan 28 1975 _____

28

# Holidays

**Punctuation Rule**: Use a comma to separate the day and year when writing a date.

Use a calendar to find the following dates for this year. Write the date on the line, using a comma to separate the day and year. _____

1. January ⟶ New Year's Day ⟶ *January 1, 2002* _____

2. February ⟶ Valentine's Day ⟶ _____

3. March ⟶ St. Patrick's Day ⟶ _____

4. April ⟶ April Fools' Day ⟶ _____

5. May ⟶ Mother's Day ⟶ _____

6. June ⟶ Father's Day ⟶ _____

7. July ⟶ Independence Day ⟶ _____

8. October ⟶ Halloween ⟶ _____

9. November ⟶ Thanksgiving ⟶ _____

10. December ⟶ Christmas ⟶ _____

# Favorite Places

**Punctuation Rule**: Use a comma to separate the city and state when writing them together. *Note:* Also place a comma after the state if the city and state occur in the middle of a sentence.

Place a comma in each sentence to separate the city from the state.

1. My grandmother lives in Boston Massachusetts.

2. We want to visit San Francisco California in the spring.

3. Have you ever been to Tempe Arizona to see the cactus?

4. They make many varieties of cars in Detroit Michigan.

5. We took a family vacation in Orlando Florida.

6. Can we visit our cousins in Denver Colorado?

7. They have a hot air balloon festival in Albuquerque New Mexico each year.

Use a map or atlas to find three places you would like to visit. Write a sentence to go with each city and state. Be sure to use a comma to separate each city and state.

1. _____

2. _____

3. _____

# Hello and Goodbye

**Punctuation Rule**: Use a comma after the greeting and closing in a letter.

Read the letter below. Place a comma after the greeting and the closing.

February 20, 2003

Dear Ben

Thank you for my cool birthday gift. I loved my super-blaster water gun and will use it often. You are a good friend.

Your pal

Colton

Place a comma after the following closings. Then add a name to the closing.

Example:   Fondly, Sarah

1. Respectfully _____   5. Yours truly _____

2. Sincerely _____   6. Sincerely yours _____

3. Best wishes _____   7. Love _____

4. With love _____   8. Your friend _____

# Quick Check #7

Correct the following sentences by adding commas and periods where they are needed.

1. My sister was born in Denver Colorado

2. She was born on July 12 1994

3. It was a warm sunny day

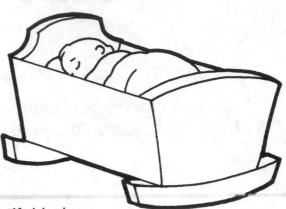

4. She weighed 7 lbs 12 oz and was a beautiful baby

5. My parents named her Kara Diane or K D for short

6. My grandma grandpa aunt and uncle came to visit her in the hospital

7. We brought her home to 8007 Linden Dr in Boulder Colorado

8. She needed a lot of tender loving care the first few months

9. She also needed lots of diapers blankets and baby food

10. She first tried to walk on June 16 1995

11. We cheered when K D finally walked her first steps

12. I love my sister my mom and my dad very much

# Quick Check #8

Read the envelope and letter below.  Place a comma wherever one is needed.

April 25 2002

Dear Tyrone

    I am writing to invite you to my birthday party.  There will be games food and drinks.  Lots of friends from class are coming.  Marcia Jim Sandy and Keith all said they could come.  My party will be at 3:00 at my house on May 7 2002.

    I hope you can come.  It would be a dull boring party without you!

Your friend

Jeremy

---

Jeremy Small

3467 Harting Pl.

Green Valley  UT  60687

Tyrone Bankston

3241 Chutley St.

New Castle UT 60543

# What Did He Say?

**Punctuation Rule**: Use quotation marks around a direct quote (words being spoken).

Use a comma to set off a quotation. Use a capital letter to begin each quotation.

Place a comma and quotation marks in each sentence below.

1. Dr. Brown said  You are fit as a fiddle!

2. Line up at the door  said Mrs. Johnson.

3. Mom yelled  Go Cobras, go!

4. Sheila wondered  Should I wear my blue dress?

5. My dad said  You look nice today.

6. James asked  Can I have a glass of milk?

7. Please answer the phone  whispered my mother.

8. Kelly exclaimed  Look out!

9. My lizard escaped, replied Henry sadly.

10. Juliette said  I hope you can come over to play.

# Speak Up

**Punctuation Rules**: Use quotation marks around a direct quote (words being spoken). Use a comma to set off a quotation. Use a capital letter to begin each quotation.

Practice using quotation marks by completing each sentence below. You can make each sentence as silly or serious as you want. Be sure to use a comma, quotation mark, and capital letter for each quotation.

1. The coach screamed _____

2. I yelled _____

3. _____ whispered the detective.

4. _____ replied the cook.

5. The doctor asked _____

6. The monster roared _____

7. _____ said our teacher.

8. The librarian said _____

# Title Time

**Punctuation Rule**: Titles found inside a book, newspaper, or magazine are written inside quotation marks. Use quotation marks around titles of magazine and newspaper articles, chapter titles, songs, and poem titles.

Circle the titles below needing quotation marks.

1. Have you finished the chapter called The Number Line in our math book?

2. We sang the song My Country 'Tis of Thee.

3. Shel Silverstein wrote a poem called The Babysitter.

4. The magazine included an interesting article called Homework Hazards.

Complete the following sentences. Be sure to use quotation marks around the names of the titles.

1. I know a song called _____ .

2. I like to read the poem titled _____ .

3. One chapter in my book is called _____ .

4. In a magazine at home there is an article titled _____ .

# Quick Check #9

Place quotation marks where they are needed in the following sentences.

1. Alysse said, Please come to my house to play.

2. Did you hear that new song called Boogie All Night Long?

3. Kick the goal! shouted the coach.

4. The first chapter of Roald Dahl's book *The Witches* is called My Grandmother.

5. Tony asked, Can I have a glass of milk with my cookies?

6. I love that new shirt with those pants, replied Heather.

7. My *National Geographic Magazine* has an article entitled The New Generation.

8. Mother said, Clean up your room before you go out to play.

9. Did you see the new *Harry Potter* movie? asked Marie.

10. The fireman shouted, Give me more hose!

# Quick Check #10

Match a quote to each speaker. Then write the sentence on the lines below. Be sure to use commas, quotation marks, and capital letters for each quotation.

| Speaker | Quote |
|---|---|
| Mother said | Let's play ball! |
| The teacher asked | Please set the table for dinner. |
| My friend shouted | Your teeth look terrific. |
| The dentist said | Do you want paper or plastic bags? |
| The grocery clerk asked | What is six times three? |

1. _____

2. _____

3. _____

4. _____

5. _____

# Correct It

Insert quotation marks, commas, periods, question marks, and exclamation points to punctuate each sentence correctly. Be sure to capitalize letters wherever needed.

1. i have a dog named butch who likes to dig roll and play fetch

2. will you come visit me in november at my house in raleigh north carolina

3. mr leeland j mathers exclaimed   I want to see that report done by tuesday

4. tiny bubbles is an old traditional song from hawaii

5. marvin t adams rode his bike to school on september 4 2000

6. dr. hutchinson asked  can i check your arms legs and feet for a rash

7. there is a tall gnarly tree outside the shop on hill st in gainstown illinois

8. on the last Friday in april we will go to the zoo museum and the park

9. while looking out the window, sheila shouted look out

10. i like the poem the homwork machine by shel silverstein

# Make No Mistake

Rewrite each sentence using the correct punctuation and capitalization.

1. i have a friend named liza who likes to eat pizza hot dogs and cookies

2. joe asked  will you go to the beach in san diego california in july

3. who let the dogs out is a popular song at the football games in dallas texas

4. did you go to the scary old house on october 31 2002

5. last saturday mr robbins shouted  go team, go

6. timothy mark and sara all live on masters rd in hartfield connecticut

# Letters

Read the following letters. Insert quotation marks, commas, periods, question marks, and exclamation points to punctuate each sentence correctly. Be sure to capitalize letters wherever needed.

may 26 2003

dear susan j hemlock

i am writing to you to introduce myself as your new pen pal    my name is janie escalle  I live at 345 jamestown st in new haven vermont  i like to bike skate and jump rope   what do you like to do  i have long brown hair and blue eyes  what do you look like  my favorite song is hit me baby one more time by brittany spears   what is your favorite song  i hope you write back soon and send me a picture of yourself  i'm so excited to be your new pen pal

sincerely

janie escalle

january 12 2003

dear grandma pat

i am so excited to come visit you march 4 2003   how is your farm on frontage rd in birmingham alabama  do you still have the cows ducks and pigs  i am looking forward to helping you paint the old red barn  will your neighbor mr brown be there to help  i told my mother that you said to come out for two weeks  when i did, my mother shouted yippee  i can't wait to see you

love

cindy

# Unit Assessment

Shade in the bubble that completes the sentence correctly.

1. Can ___ see that movie?
   - (a) i
   - (b) I
   - (c) me

2. ___ went to the beach.
   - (a) me
   - (b) i
   - (c) I

3. ___ brother has a red cap.
   - (a) My
   - (b) her
   - (c) my

4. ___ you like ice cream?
   - (a) do
   - (b) Do
   - (c) have

5. Give ___ the little car.
   - (a) john
   - (b) paul
   - (c) Marie

6. Is your dentist ___ ?
   - (a) Dr. Reed
   - (b) dr. reed
   - (c) Dr. reed

7. Can we sing on ___ ?
   - (a) Wednesday
   - (b) friday
   - (c) thursday

8. Thanksgiving is in ___ .
   - (a) november
   - (b) october
   - (c) November

9. ___ is a nice place to travel.
   - (a) arizona
   - (b) Canada
   - (c) utah

10. I like the book ___ .
   - (a) *Nova's Ark*
   - (b) *nova's Ark*
   - (c) *Nova's ark*

# Unit Assessment _(cont.)_

Shade in the bubble that completes the sentence correctly.

| | |
|---|---|
| 11. Give that to me now ___ <br> (a) . <br> (b) ? <br> (c) ! | 12. I like to eat pizza ___ <br> (a) . <br> (b) ? <br> (c) ! |
| 13. Jonathan is good at baseball ___ <br> (a) . <br> (b) ? <br> (c) ! | 14. Where is the office ___ <br> (a) . <br> (b) ? <br> (c) ! |
| 15. When will the movie begin <br> (a) . <br> (b) ? <br> (c) ! | 16. Look out for that falling rock ___ <br> (a) . <br> (b) ? <br> (c) ! |
| 17. I get shots from ___ Smith. <br> (a) Dr. <br> (b) mr. <br> (c) dr. | 18. She lives on Baker ___ <br> (a) ave. <br> (b) St. <br> (c) blvd. |
| 19. I bought one ___ donuts. <br> (a) in. <br> (b) doz. <br> (c) Mr | 20. Turn to ___ 45. <br> (a) pg. <br> (b) doz. <br> (c) Jr. |

# Unit Assessment *(cont.)*

Shade in the bubble that completes the sentence correctly.

21. Tony likes to play ____ .
    ⓐ soccer baseball and hockey
    ⓑ soccer, baseball, and hockey
    ⓒ soccer baseball, and hockey

22. Do you have ___ markers?
    ⓐ red, yellow, and blue
    ⓑ red, yellow, and, blue
    ⓒ red yellow and blue

23. The man has a ___ .
    ⓐ red shiny car
    ⓑ red, shiny, car
    ⓒ red, shiny car

24. We made lemonade with ___ .
    ⓐ sour, yellow lemons
    ⓑ sour, yellow, lemons
    ⓒ sour yellow lemons

25. I live in ___ .
    ⓐ Westminster, California
    ⓑ westminster, California
    ⓒ Westminster California

26. We visited ___ .
    ⓐ honolulu, hawaii
    ⓑ Honolulu, Hawaii
    ⓒ Honolulu Hawaii

27. She said, ___
    ⓐ I have a red ball.
    ⓑ "I have a red ball."
    ⓒ "i have a red ball."

28. Mr. Brown said, ___
    ⓐ "kick that ball!"
    ⓑ Kick that ball!
    ⓒ "Kick that ball!"

29. My favorite song is ___ .
    ⓐ jingle bells
    ⓑ Jingle Bells
    ⓒ "Jingle Bells"

30. Chapter 3 is titled ___ .
    ⓐ "Motion of the Ocean"
    ⓑ "motion of the ocean"
    ⓒ Motion of the Ocean

# Unit Assessment *(cont.)*

Read the following letters. Shade in the bubble that states the correct greeting, closing, and date.

---

31. ⓐ january 4 2002
    ⓑ January 4, 2002
    ⓒ january 4, 2002

32. ⓐ Dear Sam,
    ⓑ Dear Sam
    ⓒ dear Sam,

I am writing to thank you for your nice gift. It was very kind and thoughtful.

33. ⓐ sincerely,
    Tom
    ⓑ Sincerely,
    Tom
    ⓒ Sincerely
    Tom

---

34. ⓐ October 13, 2001
    ⓑ October 13 2001
    ⓒ october 13, 2001

35. ⓐ Dear mrs. frost
    ⓑ Dear Mrs. Frost,
    ⓒ Dear Mrs. Frost

I am writing to let you know that I won't be able to come to your party on Friday. It was kind of you to invite me. I'm sorry, but I have other plans.

36. ⓐ Yours Truly
    Mrs. Sarah Jones
    ⓑ yours truly,
    Mrs. Sarah Jones
    ⓒ Yours truly,
    Mrs. Sarah Jones

# Answer Key

**Page 5**

All answers are "I."

**Page 6**

1. Can I play on the slide today?
2. I will come back after I finish my lunch.
3. When will I get a turn on the swings?
4. I like to dig in the sand before I leave.
5. Today I had fun at the park, and I hope to come back.

**Page 7**

1. A
2. There
3. He
4. My
5. Do

**Page 8**

Order may vary.

1. My dog had puppies last year.
2. She practices playing the piano each day.
3. That duck can swim quickly.
4. Do you know how to cook?

**Page 9**

1. incorrect, My
2. correct
3. correct
4. incorrect, Do
5. incorrect, We, I
6. correct
7. incorrect, I, I
8. incorrect, We
9. correct
10. incorrect, Next, I

**Page 10**

1. I like to pretend that I can travel through time.
2. Once I pretended to visit a king and queen.
3. They took me to their castle where I met a dragon.
4. The dragon was friendly, so I named him Norbert.
5. Norbert and I flew around the kingdom in the sky.
6. What do you like to pretend?

**Page 11**

Order may vary.

Check to make sure all names are capitalized.

**Page 12**

Sentences may vary. Check to make sure names of days are capitalized and sentences are complete.

1. I had my birthday on a Tuesday in December.
2. We will take a trip on Monday in June.
3. I saw a football game on a Friday in October.

**Page 13**

Order may vary.

1. Indiana
2. Alameda Street
3. Snake River
4. Canada
5. Mount Everest
6. San Francisco
7. King Road
8. Florida
9. New Mexico

**Page 14**

1. Our class went to see *The Music Man*.
2. We read *Arrow to the Sun* to study Native Americans.
3. My favorite book is *Harry Potter and the Sorcerer's Stone*.
4. *Snow White* is now out on video.
5. I like to watch *Pokémon* on Saturday mornings.

**Page 15**

November, Dear, Sandra, I, Friday, December, It, The, Calaveras Park, Carlsbad, California, I, Your, Molly Adler

1. Dear Grandma Martha,
2. Dear Aunt Teresa,
1. Yours truly,
2. Sincerely yours,

**Page 17**

1. Jasmeet Najeed sits next to me at Kelly School.
2. We go to Hope Park after school with Jason and Kaitlin Thomas.
3. In October the leaves begin to turn red in Vermont.
4. Can you come to my house to read Goosebumps on Tuesday?
5. Mrs. Jacobs taught us to sing "This Land Is Your Land" on Thursday.
6. I love to swim with Tony and Anna in July at the Newcastle Pool.

**Page 18**

1. The cat chased a mouse.
2. My sister ate a bag of chips.
3. The hiker climbed the tall hill.
4. An old man came to my house.
5. The pink pig rolled in the mud.
6. There was a spider hanging from its web.

**Page 21**

1. St.
2. yd.
3. in.
4. Wed.
5. Dr.
6. Mr.
7. Ave.
8. Sept.
9. ft.
10. doz.

**Page 22**

Mr., K., S., Rd., Ste., CA, Dr., J., St., Blvd., Apt., ID

1. CA
2. Blvd.
3. Dr.
4. Apt.
5. ID
6. Rd.
7. Ste.
8. S.
9. St.
10. Mr.

Bonus: CA, ID

# Answer Key *(cont.)*

**Page 23**
1. Will Mr. Hall see Dr. Hay today?
2. Bill W. Hood lives on Baker St.
3. Look out for that falling tree!
4. Does Mrs. J.G. Smith have a pet poodle?
5. We won the game!
6. Will we play at the park on Hope Ave.?
7. Jr. Jones played ball on Conger Blvd.

**Page 24**

Dec. 3, 2002

Dear Samantha,

I am writing to invite you to a party for Mrs. Allen, our teacher. The party will be on Sat., Dec. 11, 2002. It will be held at my house which is located at 7008 Lantana Ave. in Wellmington. The party will start at 2:00. Do you think you can come?

We are planning to surprise Mrs. Allen with dessert, games, and a gift for being such a good teacher. Could you please bring some punch and some cups? I hope you can come. This will be the best party ever!

Your friend,

Molly S. Brown

Molly S. Brown
7008 Lantana Ave.
Wellmington, CO 80406

Samantha H. Sonnich
2437 Hanson Pl.
Wellmington, CO 80406

**Page 25**
1. pizza, pasta, or steak
2. soccer, golf, and tennis
3. red, blue, and green
4. lions, tigers, and bears
5. triangle, square, or circle
6. Monday, Friday, and Sunday

**Page 27**
2. wet, pink tongue
3. sharp, new, yellow pencil
4. big, shiny, new car
5. big, hairy, red monster
6. old, torn jeans
7. large, hot, cheese pizza
8. large, brown, fuzzy mustache
9. round, blue ball
10. red, juicy apples

**Page 28**
2. July 12, 1994
3. June 22, 1939
4. April 16, 2018
5. January 27, 1785
6. May 26, 2002
7. Aug. 13, 1875
8. Oct. 31, 1998
9. Mar. 23, 2000
10. Sept. 3, 2003
11. Nov. 15, 1793
12. Jan. 28, 1975

**Page 30**
1. Boston, Massachusetts
2. San Francisco, California
3. Tempe, Arizona
4. Detroit, Michigan
5. Orlando, Florida
6. Denver, Colorado
7. Albuquerque, New Mexico

**Page 31**

Dear Ben,

Your pal,

Add a comma and name to each

**Page 32**
1. My sister was born in Denver, Colorado.
2. She was born on July 12, 1994.
3. It was a warm, sunny day.
4. She weighed 7 lbs. 12 oz. and was a beautiful baby.
5. My parents named her Kara Diane or K.D. for short.
6. My grandma, grandpa, aunt, and uncle came to visit her in the hospital.
7. We brought her home to 8007 Linden Dr. in Boulder, Colorado
8. She needed a lot of tender, loving care the first, few months.
9. She also needed lots of diapers, blankets, and baby food.
10. She started to walk on June 16, 1995.
11. We cheered when K.D. finally walked her first steps.
12. I love my sister, my mom, and my dad very much.

**Page 33**

April 25, 2002

Dear Tyrone,

games, food, and drinks

Marcia, Jim, Sandy, and Keith

May 7, 2002

dull, boring party

Your friend,

Green Valley, UT

New Castle, UT

**Page 34**
1. Dr. Brown said, "You are fit as a fiddle!"
2. "Line up at the door," said Mrs. Johnson.
3. Mom yelled, "Go Cobras, go!"
4. Sheila wondered, "Should I wear my blue dress?"
5. My dad said, "You look nice today."
6. James asked, "Can I have a glass of milk?"
7. "Please answer the phone," whispered my mother.
8. Kelly exclaimed, "Look out!"
9. "My lizard escaped," replied Henry sadly.
10. Juliette said, "I hope you can come over to play."

**Page 36**
1. "The Number Line"
2. "My Country 'Tis of Thee"
3. "The Babysitter"
4. "Homework Hazards"

# Answer Key (cont.)

**Page 37**
1. Alysse said, "Please come to my house to play."
2. Did you hear that new song called "Boogie All Night Long"?
3. "Kick the goal!" shouted the coach.
4. The first chapter of Roald Dahl's book *The Witches* is called "My Grandmother."
5. Tony asked, "Can I have a glass of milk with my cookies?"
6. "I love that new shirt with those pants," replied Heather.
7. My *National Geographic Magazine* has an article entitled "The New Generation."
8. Mother said, "Clean up your room before you go out to play."
9. "Did you see the new *Harry Potter* movie?" asked Marie.
10. The fireman shouted, "Give me more hose!"

**Page 38**
Order may vary.
1. Mother said, "Please set the table for dinner."
2. The teacher asked, "What is six times three?"
3. My friend shouted, "Let's play ball!"
4. The dentist said, "Your teeth look terrific."
5. The grocery clerk asked, "Do you want paper or plastic bags?"

**Page 39**
1. I have a dog named Butch who likes to dig, roll, and play fetch.
2. Will you come visit me in November at my house in Raleigh, North Carolina?
3. Mr. Leeland J. Mathers exclaimed, "I want to see that report done by Tuesday!"
4. "Tiny Bubbles" is an old, traditional song from Hawaii.
5. Marvin T. Adams rode his bike to school on September 4, 2000.
6. Dr. Hutchinson asked, "Can I check your arms, legs, and feet for a rash?"
7. There is a tall, gnarly tree outside the shop on Hill St. in Gainstown, Illinois.
8. On the last Friday in April we will go to the zoo, museum, and park.
9. While looking out the window, Sheila shouted, "Look out!"
10. I like the poem "The Homework Machine" by Shel Silverstein.

**Page 40**
1. I have a friend named Liza who likes to eat pizza, hot dogs, and cookies.
2. Joe asked, "Will you go to the beach in San Diego, California, in July?"
3. "Who Let the Dogs Out" is a popular song at the football games in Dallas, Texas.
4. Did you go to the scary, old house on October 31, 2002?
5. Last Saturday Mr. Robbins shouted, "Go team, go!"
6. Timothy, Mark, and Sara all live on Masters Rd. in Hartfield, Connectiucut.

**Page 41**
May 26, 2003
Dear Susan J. Hemlock,
I am writing to you to introduce myself as your new pen pal. My name is Janie Escalle. I live at 345 Jamestown St. in New Haven, Vermont. I like to bike, skate, and jump rope. What do you like to do? I have long, brown hair and blue eyes. What do you look like? My favorite song is "Hit Me, Baby, One More Time" by Brittany Spears. What is your favorite song?
I hope you write back soon and send me a picture of yourself. I'm so excited to be your new pen pal!
Sincerely,
Janie Escalle

January 12, 2003

Dear Grandma Pat,
I am so excited to come visit you March 4, 2003! How is your farm on Frontage Rd. in Birmingham, Alabama? Do you still have the cows, ducks, and pigs? I am looking forward to helping you paint the old, red barn. Will your neighbor Mr. Brown be there to help? I told my mother that you said to come out for two weeks. When I did, my mother shouted, "Yippee!" I can't wait to see you.
Love,
Cindy

**Page 42**

| | | | | |
|---|---|---|---|---|
| 1. | b | | 6. | a |
| 2. | c | | 7. | a |
| 3. | a | | 8. | c |
| 4. | b | | 9. | b |
| 5. | c | | 10. | a |

**Page 43**

| | | | | |
|---|---|---|---|---|
| 11. | c | | 16. | c |
| 12. | a | | 17. | a |
| 13. | a | | 18. | b |
| 14. | b | | 19. | b |
| 15. | b | | 20. | a |

**Page 44**

| | | | | |
|---|---|---|---|---|
| 21. | b | | 26. | b |
| 22. | a | | 27. | b |
| 23. | c | | 28. | c |
| 24. | a | | 29. | c |
| 25. | a | | 30. | a |

**Page 45**

| | | | | |
|---|---|---|---|---|
| 31. | b | | 34. | a |
| 32. | a | | 35. | b |
| 33. | b | | 36. | c |